GEMINI

GEMINI
May 21–June 21

NAME

SUN SIGN

MOON SIGN

RISING SIGN

Crystal Astrology for Modern Life

SANDY SITRON

CONTENTS

CRYSTALS, ASTROLOGY AND YOU

8
The Stones, The Signs and You

10
The Stones

12
Your Crystal Toolkit

16
The Signs

20
Tools for Your Journey

24
Ways to Work With Crystals

UNDERSTANDING GEMINI

30
Your Sign, Explained

36
Gemini Sun

40
Gemini Moon

41
Gemini Rising

42
Other Gemini Support Crystals

43
Gemini x Love

44
Gemini x Friendship

45
Gemini x Money

46
Gemini x Work

47
Gemini x Health

GEMINI THROUGHOUT THE YEAR

50
Aries Season

52
Taurus Season

54
Gemini Season

56
Cancer Season

58
Leo Season

60
Virgo Season

62
Libra Season

64
Scorpio Season

66
Sagittarius Season

68
Capricorn Season

70
Aquarius Season

72
Pisces Season

LUNAR ENERGY AND MERCURY IN MOTION

76
The Lunar Cycle

86
Mercury Retrograde

90
Conclusion

91
Resources

95
Featured Crystals

CRYSTALS, ASTROLOGY AND YOU

THE STONES,
THE SIGNS AND YOU

The stars above you and the stones beneath your feet are part of the fabric of your world. Astrology offers a cosmic perspective. Crystals radiate with the healing energy of the Earth. Together, they serve as guides in your life, engaged in a vibrational conversation that can help you reflect on, and tune into, who you are. Birthstones and other crystals can be used to highlight and harness the energy of your astrological birth chart.

As above, so below – harness the power of crystals and the cosmos to create a deeper connection with yourself for a confident, empowered, high-vibe life.

Astrology is the ancient study of the changing positions and alternating energy of the celestial bodies and how this relates to our lives on Earth. The unique cosmic environment that you synced up with at the moment of your first breath provides awareness of – and offers a way to interpret – your personality traits, core strengths, growth areas, emotional style and so much more. When you better understand your vibrational self, it's easier to make informed choices about the big and small things in your life. Your conscious perspective is uplifted. Your mind is opened and activated.

Crystals, or 'stones', vibrate with the breath of the Earth. They act on an energetic level, sending vibrations out into the world. They are natural amplifiers of positive energy and bring discordant energies into balance. Each crystal has its own energy blueprint, which is why different types of stones may influence the human energy field in different ways. Pairing the insight that you gain from astrology with the healing power of crystals can help you navigate certain life areas and facilitate personal transformation and spiritual growth throughout the astrological year.

Crystals and the constellations call to us. In this book you'll receive a bespoke selection of crystals to help you amplify or balance the unique energies of your sign. You'll gain insight into your life, activate your highest potential and learn to live harmoniously with the energy that surrounds you.

When gazing at the night sky, when you hold a crystal in your hand, feel inspired to slow down, be present in the moment and get ready to embark on a meaningful journey of self-discovery.

YOUR UNIQUE RECOMMENDATIONS

We all accept that different things work for different people. Advice that's a perfect fit for one person might fall flat for someone else. Regardless of where Gemini sits in your personal astrology, this book will help you understand your Gemini nature and give you specific crystal recommendations for your sign and each astrological season. You can use these bespoke Gemini crystals to build confidence, spark creativity, feel more present, harmonize relationships, attract love, embrace your emotions, cultivate friendships, create abundance, optimize your health and wellness, and amplify your natural gifts.

YOUR ASTRO-CRYSTAL JOURNEY

Once you understand how the two energetic studies of crystals and astrology relate to your life, you'll be ready to take a deep dive into your Gemini energy and learn to use crystals to leverage the strengths of your Gemini gifts, whether Gemini is your Sun, Moon or Rising sign, or elsewhere in your unique astrology. You'll also discover your unique Gemini crystal recommendations for love, friendship, money, work and health to help you connect to your true potential and reach your dreams and goals.

As each astrological season holds a different kind of energy, this book will take you through the year and show you how crystals can help you channel your unique Gemini energy under each sign. In this way, you will learn to navigate through the seasons with ease and to harmonize with the cycles of nature. You will discover how crystals can help you embrace the ebb and flow of the 29-day Moon cycle, enable you to sail through Mercury Retrograde and even plan your week.

This book is part of a series that unites each of the twelve zodiac signs with recommended crystals. When you are ready to go deeper on your astro-crystal journey, you may choose to purchase the companion books in the series that correspond to the other prominent signs in your birth chart.

THE
STONES

Dazzling gemstones are typically formed deep under the Earth's surface, stimulated by the combination of mineral-rich water, heat and pressure. Subterranean 'gardens' nurture the formation of billions of atoms into highly ordered, three-dimensional repeating patterns to create unique crystals, each one holding a vibrational record of earthly, physical reality.

Across the world and over millennia, people have been fascinated by crystals. Lucent jewels have captured the imagination for over 30,000 years. In the Democratic Republic of the Congo, small tools decorated with Quartz have been found that date back to 33,000 BCE. The Ancient Sumerians of Mesopotamia (present-day Iraq) used crystals for rituals and magic in the fourth century BCE. Humankind has used crystals for decoration, status, currency, religion, healing, magic-making and, in more recent times, modern technology. Early radios used crystals as electrical and tuning components. Today's computers, LCD screens and some batteries rely on crystal technology.

Good Vibrations   People across different cultures and generations have turned to crystals as guides or helpers because it seems that, whatever facet of earthly experience you are struggling with, there is a crystal frequency that can help you move forwards on your path. Crystals may help bring calm and heal stress, empower you when you need support or confidence, or provide focus and clarity when you're struggling with an important decision. Crystals are thought to absorb the energy that you are trying to release and release the energy you are trying to absorb.

For example, if you are feeling dull and listless, Carnelian may share with you a vibration of high energy and drive. If you are overheated or stressed, Rose Quartz may help you soften and relax. Choosing the right crystal that resonates with, or reacts to, your energy can shift your mood or your mindset.

CHOOSING YOUR CRYSTALS

In Part Two of this book, you will be guided to a selection of crystals that are energetically aligned with your unique astrology. If you are adding these stones to your collection, it's important to choose responsibly.

Sustainability and Ethics How did the crystal that you have in your hand make its way to you? The answer to this question is incredibly important to the well-being of humanity and the Earth.

The crystal industry is shrouded in mystery and plagued by bad practices. When you purchase a crystal, make sure to find gems that have a traceable, and short, journey from the mine to your hand. It's important to know if the mine that the crystal came from uses ethical, safe and sustainable practices. Discover if the lapidary, where the crystal was cut and polished, is a safe place that pays a living wage to the people who work there. The easiest way to do this is to mindfully source your crystals from sellers who have done the legwork. You vote with your financial choices. Make sure that you are contributing to better health and safety for all.

More information about sustainable and ethical practices and surveyors can be found on my website www.sandysitron.com/crystals.

Size, Finish and Price When harnessing the power of a crystal for personal use, the size of the stone doesn't matter. If you are holding a crystal or carrying it close to your body, its vibration is in your energy field and will have an effect whatever its size.

A raw stone is a stone that is untreated. These are just as effective to use in healing practices as a crystal that has been tumbled or polished. So when you are choosing a crystal, choose one that appeals to you, no matter the size or finish.

The stones selected in this book can be sourced at an affordable price. Although some of the stones mentioned may sound ultra-luxurious and expensive, these stones are available at a range of values.

YOUR CRYSTAL
TOOLKIT

In the next section, you'll find crystal recommendations for your specific sign. First, here are a few indispensable crystals to round out your toolkit. These selections are a wonderful support for anyone at any time.

GROUNDING AND PROTECTION

Smoky Quartz Getting grounded is the basis of spiritual work. So many factors in everyday life pull us out of ourselves. Spending too much time on your phone, not enough time in nature or eating too much sugar are common culprits, but the list goes on. If you want to nail your next meeting at work, remember where your keys are, or get on top of that to-do list, you need to get grounded. Feeling grounded also allows you to be present in your relationships and tuned in to your physical needs. This is where Smoky Quartz can help. This crystal keeps you centred, and emotionally clear. It may help you take a more practical view of a situation. On a more mystical level, Smoky Quartz has the effect of protecting you from energetic drains on your system. It is an excellent protection stone and just holding it can help you feel steady.

CLEANSING YOUR ENERGY

Selenite Just as you bathe your body regularly, it makes sense to regularly cleanse your energy system too. Energetic cleansing can help you balance your emotions and clear your mind. Cleanse your energy after work, socializing or spending time in a crowd. Or employ Selenite to help you get rid of emotional residue after a tough conversation. Energy cleansing is also recommended when you are going through any kind of transition – a break-up, a move or some other important milestone. Use Selenite with the intention of purifying your energy field and cleansing yourself of anything that is dragging you down. Imagine that it shines a ray of light through your entire body, clearing and cleansing.

Smoky Quartz Ritual	Selenite Ritual
Perform the grounding practice on page 26 while holding Smoky Quartz to anchor you.	Selenite can also be used to cleanse the energy of your other stones. Place a Selenite stone next to your crystals overnight.

SOOTHING RELAXATION

Rose Quartz   We all know what it's like to get stressed out and frazzled. Sometimes the nervous system is overloaded and it's hard to calm down. When that happens, you need a soothing crystal ally that can help you relax. If you are having trouble sleeping, are feeling on edge, or are working through some challenging emotions, it's time to soften with Rose Quartz. This dreamy pink stone is known for its inherent ability to calm and reassure. It soothes you while strengthening your capacity for empathy and compassion. If you're feeling down, lonely or heartbroken, let this crystalline stress-reliever support you.

FINDING YOUR DIRECTION

Clear Quartz   Clear quartz is a true all-purpose stone. When you actively set an intention with Clear Quartz, the stone will magnify that intention. When your world is changing around you and you need to forge ahead in a new direction, Clear Quartz will get you there. Clear Quartz can help you clarify, strategize and set your aspirations for your life. Once programmed with your wishes and desires, this powerful amplifier will hold the vibration of your intentions and help you visualize and realize your future.

Rose Quartz Ritual	Clear Quartz Ritual
Infuse a tumbled Rose Quartz stone in your next cup of tea or glass of water for a mindful moment with a soothing elixir.	Write an affirmation that inspires you. Say your affirmation aloud while holding Clear Quartz.

Amethyst Your intuition is your natural guidance system. It's that gut feeling you have when something feels wrong, or when something feels just right. Intuition shows up in different ways for everyone but it's like a muscle that can be strengthened. If you have questions about your life and you want to tune into the answers, Amethyst is at your service. In those moments, practice asking and listening and let this violet stone help open up your mind's eye. Amethyst is also a fantastic friend when you need help saying the right thing in your next important conversation, meeting or presentation. Or if you are looking for a sparkling boost to your creativity, open the channels of inspiration with Amethyst by your side.

Amethyst
Ritual

The next time you have a question about your life or
path, lie down and place an Amethyst stone on your forehead or
near the crown of your head. Meditate and make space for
the answer to come through.

THE SIGNS

ASTROLOGY AND YOU

You are a unique being, made up of a solar system of characteristics that define your identity. Astrology illuminates your personality and your path. It describes how you think, learn, love, act and much more. Astrology can also be used to understand the energy of the moment.

Astrology has been contributed to by cultures throughout the world over thousands of years. The astrology used in this book is drawn from contemporary Western astrology. Like all things in the universe, the movements of the planets through the zodiac create a vibration. At the moment of your first breath, this energy is mirrored within you.

Your astrology is much more complex than just your star sign. The movements of the planets under the zodiac, in the exact place, at the exact moment you were born form your birth chart, a personalized map of the sky from your unique vantage point on Earth when you took your first breath. As well as showing you where the Sun lands in your chart, denoting your star sign, it also shows under which signs the Moon and other planets fall – this is the key to understanding your personal energetic code.

In order to discover your unique astrological make-up first you need to map your birth chart.

SUN, MOON AND RISING SIGN

When someone asks, 'What's your sign?' they are actually referring to your Sun sign, but it's worth learning your Moon and Rising signs too. These three symbols are a good place to begin your astrological journey as they represent the basic outline of who you are – like a simple sketch that captures your likeness in just a few brushstrokes. Together these three symbols make up your inner and outer self.

Casting Your Birth Chart Go to www.sandysitron.com/crystals and enter your birth data in the 'Create Your Birth Chart' tool. You'll then receive your birth chart, also called your natal chart, that shows the signs that the planets were in when you were born, and where they were located in the sky.

SUN
SIGN

The Sun is a constant bright light, it symbolizes your ego, the part of you that you consciously identify with. It's how you tend to think of yourself.

The Sun is the gravitational centre of the solar system, it represents your core self and describes your fundamental character and values.

The Sun is the energy source that creates life on our planet, it signifies how you channel your energy.

MOON
SIGN

The Moon is most visible at night, it symbolizes the part of you that is hard to see – your subconscious self.

The Moon changes shape through the lunar month. It represents your ever-changing emotions and how you respond subconsciously to your feelings.

The Moon is a satellite that circles the Earth, it describes how you turn inwards to protect, nurture and soothe yourself.

RISING
SIGN

· The Rising sign, also known as your Ascendant, is the constellation of the zodiac that was rising on the eastern horizon at the precise moment of your birth.

· The Rising sign shines new light into the world. It symbolizes how the rays of your personality beam out ahead as you walk down the street, meet new people, or interact on social media. It represents your vibe or your 'brand'. It epitomizes how other people see you.

· As you explore the following pages, you'll learn how to balance and enhance your unique energy using supportive crystals. Whatever your Sun, Moon or Rising sign, this book will help you find alignment and teach you how to leverage your inherent gifts.

PLANETS

SUN
☉

MOON
☽

MERCURY
☿

VENUS
♀

MARS
♂

JUPITER
♃

SATURN
♄

URANUS
♅

NEPTUNE
♆

PLUTO
♇

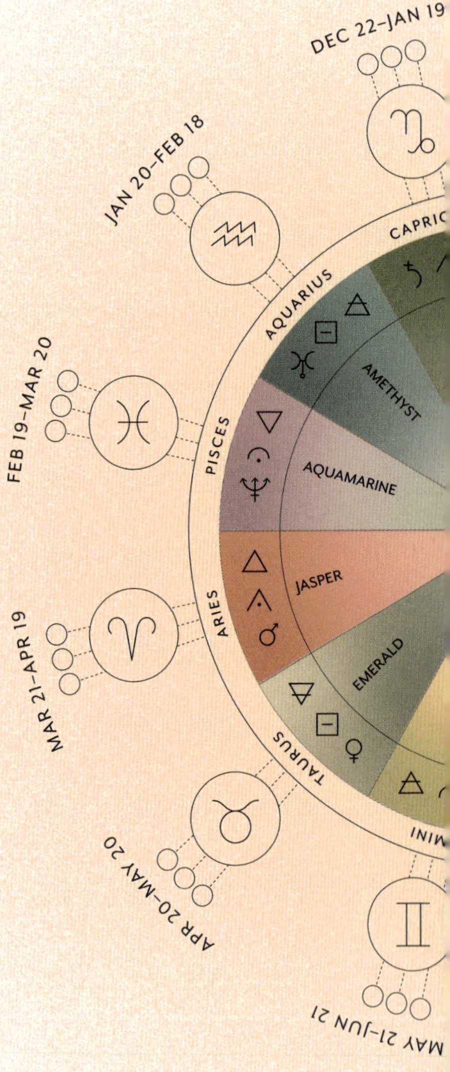

DEC 22–JAN 19
♑
CAPRICORN

JAN 20–FEB 18
♒
AQUARIUS

FEB 19–MAR 20
♓
PISCES

MAR 21–APR 19
♈
ARIES

APR 20–MAY 20
♉
TAURUS

MAY 21–JUN 21
♊
GEMINI

AMETHYST

AQUAMARINE

JASPER

EMERALD

DATES ARE APPROXIMATE AS THE DATES OF THE
SIGNS VARY BY ABOUT A DAY FROM YEAR TO YEAR.

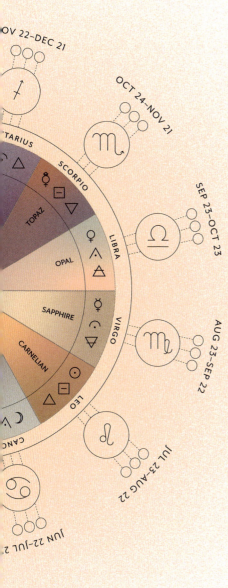

NOV 22–DEC 21

OCT 24–NOV 21

SEP 23–OCT 23

AUG 23–SEP 22

JUL 23–AUG 22

JUN 22–JUL 2?

SAGITTARIUS

SCORPIO

TOPAZ

OPAL

LIBRA

SAPPHIRE

VIRGO

CARNELIAN

LEO

CANCER

ELEMENTS

FIRE

△

EARTH

▽

AIR

△

WATER

▽

MODALITY

CARDINAL

∧

FIXED

⊟

MUTABLE

⌒

TOOLS FOR
YOUR JOURNEY

As you go forwards on your astro-crystal journey,
two key tools can help you gain insight and create positive
change – intuition and intention. Intuition helps you know
what you want and intention helps you make it happen.

LETTING YOUR
INTUITION GUIDE YOU

Everyone is intuitive, your intuition or 'inner knowing' is your built-in guidance system. Use the following prompts to strengthen your inner voice.

How to Connect with Your Intuition

Slow down Take a few deep breaths and close your eyes. The more you can slow down in your life (even for just five minutes) the louder your intuitive voice grows.

Pose a question What do you want to know? Ask yourself. Say it aloud or ponder it silently. Or choose to write it down, sketch it or even dance it out. However you pose the question, make sure it is clear. If you aren't sure what to ask, try, 'what do I need to know that I don't yet know?'

Listen for the answer You might hear words or notice a sensation in your body. You might write down your question in a notebook then flip the page and write down the answer. You might have an emotional response or feel compelled to move in a certain way. Pay attention.

Practice The more you practice asking and listening, the more you get to understand your unique intuitive voice. Just as weightlifting tones your physical body, practicing these steps improves your intuitive muscle, so stick with it!

INTENTION SETTING

In your meditations and rituals, you can program your crystals with the intentions or affirmations that will help you meet your goals.

An intention is a new thought that you would like to think. Our subconscious minds save energy by putting certain thoughts and habits on repeat. This survival skill has benefits, such as giving us more energy and space for other things, but it also has its downsides, such as getting us stuck in a negative pattern. One way to break in a new way of thinking is to intentionally repeat a new thought. Here is how to 'affirm' your new way of thinking into being!

Define what it is you would like to change. Where are you feeling stuck? What is the pattern that is bugging you? For example, 'I am stuck because I have these exciting ideas for new projects, but I never finish what I start.'

Decide what you want
For instance, 'It would be great if I finished my projects.'

Make it an 'I' statement
Such as, 'I finish my projects.'

Make it affirmative
Make sure your affirmation is positively stated. Say what you want, not what you don't want. So 'I finish my projects' not 'I no longer leave my projects unfinished'.

Make it in the here and now
Write your affirmation in the present tense: 'I finish my projects' rather than 'I will finish my projects'.

Describe the feeling
Include some positive descriptors, so that you can easily visualize how great it feels to realize your affirmation: 'I finish my projects and I feel so satisfied.'

• Evaluate Does the affirmation you wrote give you a positive feeling? If so, wonderful! You have your affirmation. If not, refine it. You may need a 'stepping stone' to make your affirmation more believable. For example, if you have a complicated track record with finishing what you begin, your subconscious mind may need more help believing 'I finish my projects and I feel so satisfied'. In that case try, 'I believe in the possibility that I finish my projects and feel satisfied', or 'I'm learning to finish my projects with satisfaction and ease'. With time and practice you'll find that you no longer need the stepping stone and you can update your affirmation to 'I easily finish my projects and I'm filled with satisfaction!'

WAYS TO WORK WITH CRYSTALS

Crystals are a powerful force as they are but, in order to optimize their benefits, discover how to care for and recharge them with regular cleansing, and learn how to activate them using the intentions you've developed.

CLEANSE YOUR
CRYSTALS

Everything on Earth must go through a process of decay and renewal. Cleansing your crystals can help them reset with a clear energetic frequency. When you cleanse a crystal, imagine that you are clearing it of any energy that it may have picked up from yourself, other people and the environment.

How to Cleanse
Your Crystals

Make sure to research your stone to discover if the method you are considering is safe for both you and the crystal. For example, some crystals may dissolve in water or fade in sunlight. Some stones contain trace minerals that may be physically harmful when released into water.

Light: Place your crystal in sunlight or moonlight for an hour.
Salt: Immerse your crystal in salt for about five minutes.
Sound: Chant or use an instrument such as singing bowls, chimes or tuning forks.
Water: Wash your crystal under running water, from a natural water source or a tap, for a few minutes.
Visualization: Imagine crystalline light or archangels surrounding your crystal with the intention of cleansing.
Selenite: Place selenite next to your crystal and leave in place overnight.
Earth: Bury your crystal underground for about a day.

When to cleanse your crystals

It's a good idea to cleanse your crystal when you first get it and about once a month after that. Cleanse more often if you use your crystals regularly.

GROUND
YOURSELF

Before you do any kind of energy work, it's
important to get grounded. When a ship puts down
its anchor in a quiet harbour, it's protected from
being pulled by strong waves back into the sea. As
you engage in energy work with crystals, you may
drift and dream far afield. It protects you to have an
anchor that keeps you connected to the Earth.

How to Get
Grounded

- To begin, set yourself up in a quiet
  and comfortable space, either
  seated or lying down. Close your
  eyes. Imagine that your torso is
  like a tree trunk with roots growing
  down through your feet.

- Breathe comfortably and deeply
  as you imagine your roots flowing
  down through the ground and all
  the way to the Earth's core.

- Visualize a healing light moving up
  through your roots into your body.
  Imagine this healing light circulating

through your body and carrying any
tension or stress away and out, and
back down into the Earth.

- Continue to imagine the energy
  flow – grounding energy coming up
  through your roots, tension and stress
  flowing back down to the Earth.

- When you feel relaxed and
  grounded, give thanks to the Earth
  before you open your eyes.

ACTIVATE YOUR CRYSTALS

Now that your crystal is cleansed and you are grounded, you can 'program' your crystal with the intention you've developed. Programming your crystal is one way to activate it so that its vibrations are attuned to your desires and goals. It's as simple as telling your crystal what you intend to create or achieve.

How to Program Your Intention

To amplify your crystal's power, focus our thoughts on your intention and ain that energy towards your crystal.

Make sure you have a clear intention or affirmation.

Set a timer for ten minutes.

Sit comfortably either in a chair or on the floor.

Hold your crystal or place it on your body. You could also place it on the floor or on a table in front of you.

- On each inhale, repeat your intention out loud or in your mind.

- On each exhale bring your attention to your crystal.

- When you notice your attention wandering, bring your awareness back to the crystal and your breath.

- Repeat until your timer sounds.

GEMINI

DATES: MAY 21–JUNE 21 ELEMENT: AIR
MODALITY: MUTABLE PLANET: MERCURY SYMBOL: TWINS
CRYSTAL: AGATE

YOUR SIGN, EXPLAINED

Sparkling, lively, quick-witted Gemini. You buzz like a honeybee, pollinating all of the flowers in the garden. You are continually making connections by bringing a message to a neighbour, a new idea to your community, or learning something new. Your words of wisdom, gossip, spiritual messages, news, poems, writings, and speeches fill the airwaves. Your sign's motto is 'I think', representing your talents for teaching, learning, adapting and mingling with others. You are the ultimate connector, bringing together ideas and people.

Gemini is quick and loves to multitask, dipping in and out, involved in everything and traveling everywhere. Your Gemini energy shows when you adapt and change according to what the world demands of you. You are always refining your ideas and continuously educating yourself and others. The Information Age needs ideas, and you are the supplier, keeping up a quick pace.

Your communication style is dynamic and intelligent. You have a way with words, and you love to talk. Chatting with your friends is your best form of therapy. Others look to you for entertainment and fresh insights.

You are an animated and vibrant being. And you aren't afraid to put yourself out there or show off your brilliance. In fact, when you are called up to centre stage, your wit and razor-sharp communication skills shine like a beacon. Since your sign is ruled by intellectual, logical, social and talkative Mercury, you love nothing more than to dazzle others.

GEMINI IS AN AIR SIGN

r flows through and around every
eature on Earth. It is invisible but
uches everything. In astrology, the
r element symbolizes mental and
cial connections. You show up with
nversation and curiosity, ready to
scover what connects us all.

GEMINI IS A PERSONAL SIGN

s the first of the three Air signs,
emini is a Personal sign. Personal
gns encourage you to explore
thout regard to outside factors such as
her people or the world around you.
ur own mindset is something you are
rious about. And asking yourself deep
testions is both your talent and your
y to clarity.

GEMINI IS A MUTABLE SIGN

he Mutable signs adapt and refine.
his energy helps keep you on your
es, constantly improving how you
ink. Gemini is the editor of the
diac, sifting through ideas and
oving the project forward.

GEMINI IS RULED BY THE PLANET MERCURY

Mercury is the messenger planet. As
it zips through the solar system, faster
than any other planet, it seemingly
'talks' with all of the other planets.
Similarly, you might find yourself
running messages and bringing people
together through words and ideas.

THE TWINS ARE THE SYMBOL FOR GEMINI

One twin is mortal, focused on
understanding life on Earth. The
other twin is immortal, connecting to
intuition and spiritual inspiration.

AGATE IS A KEY CRYSTAL BIRTHSTONE FOR GEMINI

Agate is a calming stone. With its steady
energy, it is the perfect support for
Gemini's rambunctious and lively vibe.
This centering stone may help you relax
and focus on what's most important.
With any variety of Agate by your
side, you can slow down and ask the
questions that are most important. This
crystal helps you prioritize.

GEMINI
TRAITS

Your key traits show how you shine.
These are the special characteristics
that make you unique.

Curious You know how to ask the right questions. You love nothing more than to be informed. Your sense of wonder and curiosity helps you discover treasures in mundane moments and everyday encounters.

Social You can be outgoing, flirty, extraverted and talkative.

Communicative You understand the power of words and ideas, and you know that the delivery is important. You are the marketer among the zodiac signs, and the original storyteller too.

Open-minded You are filled with wonder and you are very accepting of others. At your core, you seek to understand, and you approach every situation with an open mind.

Quick You are lively, zippy and energetic. You're quick with a comeback and are able to do a million things at once.

Smart Sharp, brainy and clever! You pick up new things quickly. Your mind is naturally versatile and curious and you may be unusually well read.

Fun Not only are you fun, but you're funny too! Gemini is full of pep, with an upbeat personality.

Adaptable You are agile in mind and body. This helps you adapt to ever-changing circumstances. You focus on improving yourself and you are always willing to change.

GEMINI GIFTS
AND GROWTH AREAS

Your natural gifts offer both strengths and challenges. The same traits that make you special may also require balance at times.

Objective vs Subjective   When you feel opinionated, you might find it hard to be open-minded. Depending on the situation, you can be either very objective and tolerant or very subjective and judgemental.

Dazzling vs Distracted   You are one of the most dazzling and lively signs of the zodiac – you are everywhere at once. Sometimes you move so fast that it can be hard to focus on just one thing, giving you a very short attention span.

Expression vs Exaggeration A natural storyteller, you're expressive and captivating. Sometimes you exaggerate to keep your audience enraptured.

Adaptable vs Abrupt   You adapt quickly and are ready to move on to the next thing. In certain situations that can read as impulsive or abrupt.

Skilful vs Superficial   You're naturally good at almost anything. At times, you might skim the surface, instead of diving deep into one subject or speciality.

Inquisitive vs Intrusive   Your curiosity can sometimes lead you out of bounds, and at those moments you verge on being too nosy.

Compatibility is a complex feature of astrology because you are more than just your Sun sign. And other people are multi-faceted too.

Friends

Your **Aries** pals keep you on your toes, and for someone as quick and fun as you are, that's saying a lot. You love the way they inspire you to discover something new.

Leo loves to play like a kid, and you feel youthful and enthusiastic when you're basking in their fun-loving energy.

With your **Libra** pal you stay up late, talking all of your dreams and hopes into existence. The laughs you share are limitless.

You and **Aquarius** are equally inquisitive. As a dynamic pair, you'll either be making fashion statements, founding innovative start-ups or sparking revolutions.

Foes

Taurus is so practical and comfort-loving that you may find yourself sneaking out of the window at the suggestion of another night in watching movies on the couch.

Cancer will be going through the photo albums while you're out making new memories.

Scorpio can match you with inquisitiveness, but sometimes the depth of their probing will leave you squirming with discomfort.

When **Capricorn** is following traditions, you'd rather take the spontaneous approach.

| ARIES | LIBRA | TAURUS | SCORPIO |
| LEO | AQUARIUS | CANCER | CAPRICORN |

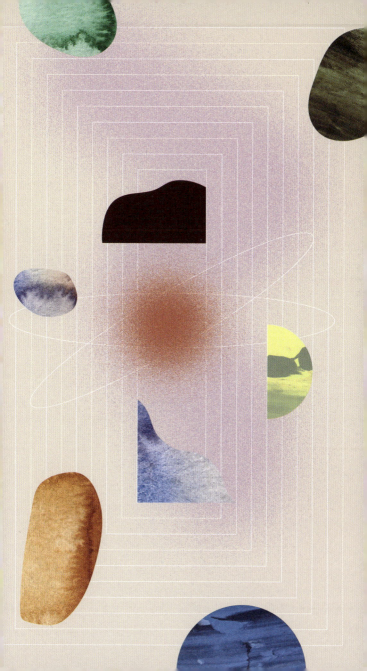

GEMINI
SUN

If you were born May 21–June 21, Gemini is your Sun sign (check your birth chart for an exact calculation). Your Sun sign describes your basic energy.

Just as the Sun is the centre of the solar system, your Sun sign (also called your zodiac sign or star sign) symbolizes the core of your being. As a Gemini Sun, you deeply value knowledge, learning and openness. You are effervescent and dynamic as you network with a constantly shifting world of people and ideas. New questions, bright ideas and friendship fuel you.

You tend to be lively and animated. This wonderful high energy can sometimes make you feel nervous or restless. If this happens, you may benefit from slowing down so that you feel steady and grounded.

Because your Sun sign fuels your confidence and enlivens your sense of self, there are two recommended crystals for Gemini Sun. The Amplifying crystal will help you expand upon your gifts and the Balancing crystal will help you integrate your growth areas.

GEMINI SUN
AMPLIFYING CRYSTAL

**COMMUNICATION, WISDOM,
INTUITION, LISTENING, CALM**

Blue Lace Agate   One way of thinking about the Gemini symbol, the Twins, is that one twin is mortal and the other immortal. The mortal twin is concerned with life on Earth, talking and listening to others, sharing thoughts and ideas. The immortal twin represents the introverted and spiritual side of Gemini, helping you connect to your inner wisdom and your higher self.

Blue Lace Agate can help you forge a relationship with both twins. This periwinkle-blue stone helps your mortal twin when you show off your mind through insightful conversation. It calms you so that you can speak and listen

clearly. When you feel calm, collected and confident, you share your brilliant self naturally, without any fear of being misunderstood. Blue Lace Agate steadies and supports you so that your unique and interesting personality is amplified.

This crystal ally connects you with your immortal twin by helping you speak with wisdom. It opens you up to the brilliance of your higher self. Keep this dazzling stone nearby when you want to go on a spiritual journey. You may like to practice a calming meditation while holding Blue Lace Agate so that you can slow down and listen to the truth in your heart.

GEMINI SUN
BALANCING CRYSTAL

**STABILITY, CALM,
CONNECTION**

Moss Agate Verdant Moss Agate is a gentle stone that can help airy Gemini energy feel settled and rooted. With a stable base, your Gemini curiosity has a safe space from which to take flight. When you need to feel settled and calm, you can also rely on Moss Agate to help you land.

You have big dreams and ideas, and Moss Agate inspires you to do the hard work necessary to make those concepts take shape. This stone offers a gentle pulse that helps you keep pushing forward.

While you are busy learning, connecting, communicating and sharing, it helps to have a crystal ally that can let you see the beauty in the moment and in yourself. Let Moss Agate allow you to slow down and soak up the wonders around you.

GEMINI MOON

PEACE,
OPPORTUNITY, LOVE

In the same way that the Moon always appears to be changing shape in the sky, the Moon in your chart symbolizes the part of you that is always changing – your emotions.

Imagine that when you have an emotion come up, the Gemini part of you steps to centre stage. This happens throughout the day. It doesn't matter if the emotion is happiness, sadness, frustration or exhilaration – when emotions arise you go into full Gemini mode. Your quick, inquisitive, analytical, communicative and distracted side is accentuated.

Your greatest wish is to be heard, seen and understood. You benefit emotionally when you are able to talk your issues out with a friend or therapist.

In intense moments of uncertainty, you feel comforted by learning as much as you can about the topic that worries you. Often, this strategy is helpful, but there may be moments when your need for information becomes obsessive. Soothe your emotions by talking yourself through your feelings logically, and taking breaks from over-thinking.

You are lively, fun, inquisitive and love to connect with others. However, your Gemini Moon can sometimes feel overstimulated. You are most supported by a crystal that centres and soothes you, while helping you nurture, and flow with, your emotions.

Chrysocolla   When your emotions swell, the harmony and sweetness of Chrysocolla can soothe you. As a Gemini Moon, you find comfort in extraverted activities, but this crystal helps you find your centre by tuning in to your inner world. Blue or Green Chrysocolla can show you that true confidence is sourced from deep within oneself.

This stone is so gentle that you may find yourself softening. It helps you tune into the abundance that is all around you and open up to new opportunities.

You thrive when you can express yourself clearly. When you have something you need to say, this peaceful crystal supports you in speaking from the heart.

GEMINI RISING

ENERGY,
CLARITY, CLEARING

our Rising sign is the sign that was
1 the eastern horizon when you were
orn. It represents the face you show
the world – your social personality.
s a Gemini Rising, you dazzle others
ith words and talents. When you
nter a room, your vibe is peppy and
netic. You seem to be everywhere at
nce. You have news, stories, insights
nd a keen sense of humour, keeping
our listeners fully enamoured. You're
so the one listening. Asking questions
one of your great skills – you know
at everyone has a story and one of the
nost fascinating parts of life is learning
om others.

Connection is the guiding
rinciple of your life. You naturally
ring others together. Not only do you
ntroduce your friend groups, socialize
nd network, but you also befriend
nany of the would-be strangers in your
eighbourhood. You know the people
ho work in every coffee shop and
orner store and they can count on you
r small talk and cheer.

As a Gemini Rising, you are
upported by a crystal that helps you

feel bright and vivacious. A crystal that
amplifies your natural vibe makes you
feel that all is well in the world.

Quartz   You love options, so choose
from a Quartz varietal such as
Rutilated Quartz, Girasol Quartz or
Clear Quartz. This abundant mineral
helps to amplify your natural Gemini
Rising gifts of sociability, intelligence
and joyfulness. Employ this stone
to energize yourself so that you can
connect honestly with others, awaken
your mind and brighten your day.

This stone helps you find the
mental clarity that you crave. Your
mind is awakened with the help of
Clear Quartz, making it a wonderful
crystal to keep by your side when
you're speaking, writing or working.

If you are feeling disconnected, or
if you're overthinking things, program
your Quartz crystal with intentions
that are designed to counterbalance
these issues.

OTHER
GEMINI
SUPPORT
CRYSTALS

The following crystals are helpful for all
Gemini placements – your Sun, Moon,
Rising Sign and any other Gemini planet or
point you may have in your chart. Harness
the potential of these stones for clarity and
ease in important life areas.

everyone has different goals for romantic love. In addition, your wishes or desires can change over time. You may wish to attract pursue love. Perhaps you are hoping deepen your ability to love, or to open to intimacy physically, emotionally or spiritually. As a Gemini, you are multi-faceted, delightful and intensely interesting. Your lover must be equally entertaining and maybe even surprising. Love is fun and playful, and you want your time together be filled with body-shaking laughs and breakthrough insights. In love, you need a crystal ally that can help you feel enlivened and to communicate the truth of your heart. You want love to satisfy your need to be understood and to feel connected.

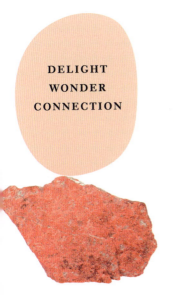

**DELIGHT
WONDER
CONNECTION**

Thulite Reach for this pale red crystal when you want to feel delighted and enlivened. Thulite helps you joyfully connect with your heart. You have a capacity to find joy in every mundane moment. When you bring this sense of wonder into your relationships, love becomes stronger. When you gaze at Thulite's soft pink colour, imagine your heart centre softening and opening. Feeling understood is the key to your Gemini heart. Let Thulite help you confidently reach out to another person. Create connections and let the love flow in.

GEMINI × FRIENDSHIP

Friends offer support, fun, love and new perspectives. With Gemini placed prominently in your chart, you live for your friendships! Your ever-expanding social circle reminds you that you're connected, and introduces you to different facets of life. You dash from party to coffee date to video call, and each encounter gives you a fresh dose of energy. For vitalized friendship, you need a crystal that helps you feel light-hearted and sincere in your social connections, so that you benefit from all the fresh energy that your community provides.

Aquamarine   You are a connector and it's easy for you to make friends and stay in touch with them. Aquamarine can help you communicate with your favourite people in a way that's non-judgemental and aligned with your highest truth. This fresh blue stone will help you speak directly from your heart. You are honest and truthful with the gift of clarity that this crystal offers. Your friendships also benefit from the gentle relaxation that Aquamarine brings. Its soothing and calming energies help you flow with whatever happens.

**CLARITY
CONNECTION
SOOTHING**

strological insight can help increase your oney-making potential. Your Gemini osperity gifts are joy, curiosity, versatility, gic, intellect and cooperation. Look to these ialities for fiscal inspiration. What stokes ur curiosity? What kind of endeavour allows u to constantly move around, work with ew people or learn new things? As a Gemini, ur money-management style needs to allow nple room for adaptation and adjustment. usterity measures won't cut it, especially there is no room in your budget for your lucation or social life – both of which are riorities for you. Financial opportunities often me through your relationships, so lean on ur community to reach your financial goals.

**JOY
IMAGINATION
CONFIDENCE**

Citrine   Citrine is a lemon-hued crystal that hits like a ray of sunshine. It may help you open up your mind to the vast potential and possibilities that are available to you. As a Gemini, you love to be mentally inspired and filled with new ideas. Citrine also helps you feel fired up and charged. You are confident and courageous with the help of Citrine. With imagination and confidence on your side, it's easy to make choices that lead to prosperity. Be creative and find inspired solutions that help you meet your financial goals with the help of Citrine.

GEMINI X WORK

When it comes to work, you're a quick learner, well-rounded, multi-talented and highly intelligent. Your ideal career provides variety and plenty of opportunities for change and growth. You excel in communications of all kinds and your social skills help with your success. Your challenge is feeling as if you are focused enough. You wonder if your knowledge could be more thorough. Throw off the artificial construct that you must be a 'specialist' at work and embrace your true talent – which is your versatility. Your best crystal ally for a vitalized career is one that helps you feel confident to be yourself.

Tiger's Eye   As a Gemini, you have a lively and versatile nature. When you need support to feel both versatile and steady, reach for Tiger's Eye. This lustrous golden and amber crystal will help you feel grounded so that you can make choices with intention. You crave confidence to be yourself and Tiger's Eye can support you with slow-burning courage. This energy helps you persevere and keep going when you might otherwise run out of steam. When there's a lot going on at work, or in your life, reach for Tiger's Eye to help you balance and centre your lively energy.

**STRENGTH
COURAGE
GROUNDING**

our friends enliven you, so count on your
social network to help you stay healthy.
Variety is good for your overall well-being.
Make your healthy habits fun, varied and
social. When you find yourself multitasking
all day long and keeping up with all the
breaking news, your nervous system takes
a hit. Quiet time and gentle breathing
techniques support you. Your diet can always
use more attention as you tend to be on-the-
go a lot, and may ignore your nutrition and
water intake. Slow down and get organized
to provide yourself with the foods that your
body needs most. Reach for a crystal that
supports you in achieving a calm, meditative
state so that you can soothe your active mind
and focus on important health habits.

**INNER WISDOM
INSIGHT
CALM**

Apophyllite   When your mind is
spinning and you can feel burnout
coming on, or you are overly worried
about something, reach for Apophyllite.
This luminous, colourless crystal can
help you connect to your inner wisdom.
Your higher self is a wonderful guide
and may help you make choices that
are aligned with your best interests.
Apophyllite holds a high vibration
that may help you release distracting
thoughts and calm your mind when
used in meditation. Tune in to your vast
inner knowledge and feel centered with
the help of Apophyllite.

GEMINI THROUGHOUT THE YEAR

he energies of the zodiac signs affect us throughout the
ar. In astrology, there is a season for everything. Feeling
parated from nature's cycles and rhythms can make you
el out of step or off-kilter. It may add to stress and drain
ergy. Understanding and attuning to astrology's seasons
ight help you feel enlivened.

Take this attunement one step further by using crystals to
nplify the unique energy of each moment, so that you feel
lly aligned with the rhythms of nature.

The following pages take you on a journey with the sun
it passes through the twelve signs of the zodiac on its
nual rotation. You will discover the key energies of each
ason, along with a sign-specific horoscope that aligns with
e important themes of your unique chart.

CONFIDENCE AND LEADERSHIP

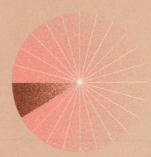

Aries season is the signal that begins the horse race.
And they're off! This is the moment to gallop at top speed
towards your goals. Put yourself out there with confidence.
Make bold decisions and step in time with your intuition.
This season is about saying YES to who you are and living
your life with freedom. The buds are beginning to emerge
and new life is beginning. Sync up with this feeling of
potential and possibility.

GEMINI HOROSCOPE FOR ARIES SEASON

Think big and imagine a fresh direction for yourself. The Sun is lighting up your zone of breakthrough ideas, community and the future. What do you want to create and who do you want to have by your side? Make time to network. Cultivate inspiring conversations. Form a mental picture of your future.

Morning Practice

Get your heart rate up with some fiery cardio exercise.

Evening Practice

Cool down that inner fire with a soothing herbal tea.

CRYSTALS FOR
ARIES SEASON

CONFIDENCE

Hessonite Garnet   Developing confidence is a practice of establishing deep self-trust. Let Hessonite Garnet's activating and powerful energy help you build up your courage so that you can just go for it. Also try Green Aventurine, Orange Calcite or Malachite.

LIVING BOLDLY

Pink Aventurine   When the time is ripe for taking bold action, Pink Aventurine can help you advance into your next adventure. Reach for it when you need a boost of fun. This spirited crystal connects you with your heart centre, and acts as your best accomplice in bravery and boldness. Or choose Ruby, Tangerine Quartz or Sardonyx.

DRIVE

Fire Agate   Aries season is the vehicle in which to follow your passions and desires, which makes Fire Agate the gasoline. Whether you need to get an important project going or just tackle spring cleaning, put yourself on track to get things done by syncing up with the vibration of this fierce crystal. You could also reach for Bloodstone, Stromatolite or Cinabrite.

MONEY AND SELF-WORTH

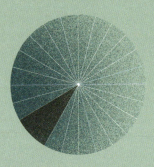

Like working in a garden and then enjoying the beauty that you've cultivated, Taurus represents sustained effort that leads to a productive reward. This season is the prime time to focus on building up your sense of personal worth and value. On one level, this process may involve nurturing your self-esteem. On another level, this may include thinking about security, money and finances. Taurus season is also a time to remember the beauty of life. It reminds us that no matter what is going on, there are simple pleasures to be had.

GEMINI HOROSCOPE FOR TAURUS SEASON

With the Sun touring your sector of dreams and intuition, it's time to retreat and listen to your heart. Let go of what you know, and open your mind to alternative ways of processing the world. Music, art, meditation, prayer . anything that helps you feel instead of think. Slow down and connect to your inner truth.

Morning Practice

Practice gratitude by reminding yourself of three things you're grateful for.

Evening Practice

Do something that feels good to your body, like stretching or wearing soft clothing.

CRYSTALS FOR TAURUS SEASON

MONEY MAGIC

Green Jade   No matter where you are beginning financially, Green Jade will juice up your money situation. This abundance stone has a way of amplifying your potential. A soft and expansive prosperity stone that soothes the spirit, it will support you as you make wise financial decisions. Reach for it when you crave a feeling of security. You could also use Pyrite, Emerald or Epidote.

SELF-WORTH

Red Jasper   Red Jasper will amp up your self-appreciation quotient. Choose Red Jasper when you're feeling uncertain, if your confidence could use a boost, or if you want to feel more resilient in any way. This stone will get you in the groove of trusting your own value. Also try Carnelian, Chrysocolla or Bixbite.

ABUNDANCE

Green Apatite   If you are feeling like something in your life is lacking, such as money, time, energy, sleep, or support, for example, you might need to boost your sense of abundance. Taurus season is the perfect time to grasp hold of that feeling of nature's plentifulness. Use Green Apatite to replenish your energy and help you feel satisfied and satiated with what you have. You could also reach for Golden Tourmaline, Uvarovite Garnet or Agate.

VALUES
AND COMMUNITY

Gemini energy is like a buzzing bee that moves from flower to flower in a garden. This season is a time of mental stimulation, new ideas, learning, communicating and sharing. Use Gemini season to evaluate or challenge your mindset and values. Which attitudes are no longer serving you? What's truly important to you? Gemini season is also a time to connect with others in the community. What can you learn from others? What can you teach others? It's a fun and lively season full of new connections.

GEMINI HOROSCOPE
FOR GEMINI SEASON

With the Sun in your zone of 'you' (aka personality and identity) it's time to express yourself. What makes you feel like you? What helps you feel lit up and joyful? Don't shrink from the spotlight. Your birthday season is the time to be unabashedly yourself and light up the room. Do your favourite things and be yourself.

Morning Practice	**Evening Practice**
Help a new mindset emerge with a potent Gemini season intention.	Before falling asleep, envision yourself having a great time at a party surrounded by everyone you love.

CRYSTALS FOR
GEMINI SEASON

MASTER YOUR MINDSET

Heliodor   Have repeating thoughts, fears or anxieties been plaguing you? Use the revitalizing energy of Gemini season and Heliodor to hit the reset button on these old thought patterns. This stone will gently help you harmonize your thoughts and adjust your mindset, helping you reconnect with your true values. Alternatively, try Blue Lace Agate, Chrome Chalcedony or Dragonstone.

CONNECTING

Agatized Coral   When you really want to feel connected, seen, heard and understood, reach for Agatized Coral. This fossilized coral nudges you to reach out to others and helps you analyse your relationships, whether with friends, lovers, family, neighbours or colleagues. It relays an upbeat feeling so that you can view your relationships with the people in your life with optimism. You may also choose Citrine, Apricot Agate or Bismuth.

COMMUNICATION

Aquamarine   Aquamarine is your crystal-clear communication companion. Communication helps us feel connected, and allows us to learn and grow. In those moments when you feel confused or foggy, this elegant stone will help you become grounded and steady. Use Aquamarine to find your voice – it will help you tune into your own true message and the truth of those around you. Alternatively, reach for Turquoise, Prairie Tanzanite or Green Chrysocolla.

HOME AND NURTURE

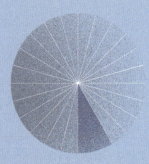

Come on home to Cancer season. Like Cancer's symbol, the Crab, wrap yourself in a protective shell and reflect on your life and your feelings. In Cancer season, engage in meaningful self-care, and also put your energy into nurturing others. Discover what makes you feel safe and cosy. This could be your actual home, your closest relationships or tending to the feelings and needs of your inner child.

GEMINI HOROSCOPE FOR CANCER SEASON

The focus is on security, money and cultivating a feeling of confidence. What makes you feel strong and stable? Although security and money can offer a sense of safety, your real confidence comes from self-trust. Look to your past experiences to shore up your belief in yourself. Trust that you have always learned what you needed to learn.

Morning Practice	Evening Practice
et your inner child take the lead: what do they want to do today?	Sing a lullaby to soothe your inner child before bed.

CRYSTALS FOR
CANCER SEASON

NURTURING

Blue Calcite   What do you want to actively care for?
Yourself? A child? A creative project? In order to feel truly
nurturing, you need to feel inspired by love. Blue Calcite will
help you soften and open up your heart centre, so that you
feel drawn to put your compassionate and attentive energy
where it is needed most. Other nurturing crystals include
Moonstone, Blue Chalcedony and Bumblebee Jasper.

HOME ENVIRONMENT

Pink Mangano Calcite   Home is where you are safe and
protected. It's your emotional nest where you can relax. Use
Pink Mangano Calcite to create a grounded and peaceful
home environment. This stone acts as a balm that will help
you feel harmonized. Place this rosy crystal in your inner
sanctum and set the intention to soothe conflict and soften
your environment so that you can restore your energy after a
long day or week. You could also try Chiastolite, Rose Quartz
or Peach Moonstone.

FAMILY BONDS

Bornite   Family, whether chosen or blood-related, represent
some of our closest relationships. Use Bornite to foster the
strength of family relationships. This is a joyful stone that
will help you embrace the positives that come from your
family circle, while at the same time grounding you to help
you remember who you are as an individual. Also try Orange
Calcite, Indigo Gabbro or Girasol Quartz.

CREATIVITY
AND FUN

Harnessing your creativity and expressing your
true self with others, that's the key to making the most of Le
season. It's all about playful sharing and creative shining.
Radiate your magnificent heart of gold outwards with
immediacy, freedom, spontaneity, generosity and a giant
sense of fun. During this season of wholehearted
self-expression, take a little time to remember how unique
you are. Remember what inspires you and reflect on what
you love most about yourself.

GEMINI HOROSCOPE
FOR LEO SEASON

Curiosity will light you up at this time.
Try learning something new or asking a
question that changes your perspective.
The Sun is currently touring your sector
of mindset, friends and communicatioı
Use this energy to open up to fresh
ideas and connect with the people whc
inspire you.

Affirmation

MY CREATIVE SELF IS
COMING OUT TO PLAY.

Morning Practice

Create daily.

Evening Practice

Seek out a chance to laugh every
day and go to bed with a smile on
your face.

CRYSTALS FOR
LEO SEASON

INSPIRATION

Rutilated Quartz Inspiration is the creative spark and
Rutilated Quartz can help you turn that spark into a roaring
bonfire. Make Leo season feel lit up with creativity. Keep
Rutilated Quartz by your side when you need an inventive
solution to a problem at work, when your love life could use
an inspiring reboot, or when you are ready to awaken the artist
within. Set your intentions and let this highly programmable
stone carry the flame of your dreams. You could also use
Sunstone, Golden Labradorite or Yellow Sapphire.

SELF-APPRECIATION

Thulite Leo season is the time to shed all insecurities and
put your faith in your one true self. Loving yourself dissolves
insecurity and self-criticism. Thulite tunes you into the
vibration of love, peace and harmony, allowing you to be
present and wholly yourself. Alternatively, reach for Ruby,
Larimar, or Desert Jasper.

COURAGE

Golden Apatite To ensure your lion-heartedness knows no
bounds, you need to fire up your courage. Golden Apatite
bestows upon you both passion and discernment, which
determine which fears are baseless. Use it when you need
to take a risk at work, strike up a conversation with someone
you admire or stand up for your values. Other courage-giving
crystals are Carnelian, Iolite-Sunstone or Citrine.

HEALTH
AND HABITS

Our goals and dreams require a big-picture view,
but Virgo season reminds us that life is actually lived in the
small details. Focus on how you are living your life, your
everyday routines and rituals. On a practical level, what is
important to you? Virgo energy helps you take a closer
look at your health and habits, and how you can be
of service to others as well.

GEMINI HOROSCOPE
FOR VIRGO SEASON

Think about what makes you feel at
home. Gain support from the loved
ones in your inner circle. The Sun is
transiting your zone of home, family
and tender emotions. If you are caught
up in the ebb and flow of feelings
more than usual right now, it's OK to
let yourself drift in the current. Follow
each emotion to its source. Give
yourself care and nurture.

Affirmation
I CREATE HEALTHY HABITS.

Morning Practice	**Evening Practice**
Drink a glass of water first thing.	Write down one task you're going to complete tomorrow, and stick to it.

FOCUS

Clear Quartz Virgo season ushers in a chance to notice the details and get focused. Use Clear Quartz to take you all the way there. This cleansing stone helps you rivet your attention on your commitments. When you program Clear Quartz with your intention for focus, you'll find that it supports you, whether you have a tight deadline or you just really need to concentrate. You could also turn to Vanadinite, Amazonite or Tiger Iron.

HEALTH

Chevron Amethyst A lot of factors go into maintaining optimum health: genetics, diet, exercise, access to care, to name just a few. Virgo season energy will encourage you to think wisely about the preventative measures that you can take to boost both your mental well-being and physical health. Use Chevron Amethyst for gentle motivation that can help you happily embrace healthier choices. Or try Girasol Quartz, Ruby Fuchsite or Black Tourmaline.

ALTRUISM

Stromatolite Humanity wouldn't be a successful species without the desire to be of service to others. Virgo season plus Stromatolite is your recommendation for kindness and selfless action. Turn your attention to what you can do to help others, whether that's volunteering, making a donation to a good cause, or simply smiling and being friendly. Let Stromatolite amplify your altruistic nature. Alternatively, reach for Stichtite, Rhodonite or Rose Quartz.

RELATIONSHIPS AND BALANCE

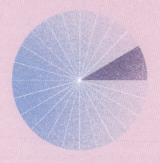

Libra season is symbolized by balanced scales. It's a chance to look at all life areas and judge the equilibrium. Are your relationships in balance? Do both people in your relationships have what they want and need? This can be a fun and harmonious time to socialize. During Libra season, balance can also be created in your environment through art, decoration and organization. The scales are the symbol for justice and Libra season brings a collective yearning to make the systems of government more fair and to expose inequalities.

GEMINI HOROSCOPE FOR LIBRA SEASON

If you need a boost of inspiration, mimic the high energy and confident playfulness of a child. You know how to have fun. And right now, the Sun is shining the spotlight on joy and creativity. Share your special sparkle with the world. And since it's Libra season, maximize your fun by getting a partner or collaborator involved in your adventures.

Morning Practice

Reach out and message
someone who is important to
you, and tell them why.

Evening Practice

Meditate to create
mental balance.

CRYSTALS FOR
LIBRA SEASON

HEALTHY BOUNDARIES

Iolite   Communicating what you want, need and desire is a
great starting point to gain clarity in your relationships. Iolite
can help you reflect and get to know yourself – the first step to
speaking and sharing your truth with others. Once your inner
base is stabilized, Iolite can help you reach out to another
person, while maintaining your own healthy boundaries. This
healing stone has a peaceful energy that helps you create
balance between yourself and a partner. You could also use
Amazonite, Purple Jade or Chiastolite.

BALANCE

Shungite   Balance is an active state, requiring constant
adjustment. It comes under the jurisdiction of the intellectual,
analytical sign of Libra. Keep checking in with yourself
throughout Libra season to determine what needs more
balance. For a crystal that will help you stay steady, reach for
Shungite. Or choose Diopside, Selenite or Turquoise.

DECISIVENESS

Ametrine   Libra season is an excellent time to analyse, think
things through and come up with new ideas. Keep Ametrine
by your desk for productive planning sessions and for when you
have big decisions to make. This balancing stone will help you
keep your life on track. As an alternative, try Variscite, Fluorite
or White Sapphire.

TRANSFORMATION
AND FORGIVENESS

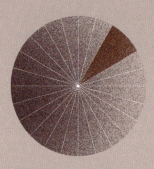

Scorpio season pulls you deeper – emotionally, physically and spiritually. This is a season of transformation, helping you to feel deeply, release old emotions and thought patterns, and get ready to move on to the next stage. By pulling back the layers and being honest with the truth of who you are, it's also an opportunity to deepen your relationships with others by letting them get to know the real you.

GEMINI HOROSCOPE
FOR SCORPIO SEASON

With the Sun in your zone of organization and healthy habits, you may feel drawn to refine and improve your life in various ways. Keep your hands busy and use this energy to get a lot done. Think about your body and take practical steps that will help you optimize your health. Simple strategie will take you far.

Morning Practice

Forgive yourself
for something.

Evening Practice

Forgive someone else
for something.

CRYSTALS FOR SCORPIO SEASON

INTIMACY

Red Tourmaline   Scorpio season propels you to create
warmth and closeness. But opening yourself up to the
vulnerability of intimacy demands courage. Whether you are
setting the stage for sexual intimacy or emotional intimacy,
Red Tourmaline will help you feel confident enough to
embrace deep connection with others. Other crystals for
intimacy are Garnet, Shiva Lingam or Red Aventurine.

TRANSFORMATION

Moldavite   Transformation brings both endings and
new beginnings. Moldavite will help you spiritually and
emotionally adjust when change comes into your life – when
a relationship has run its course, a shift is needed in the
work arena or a new adventure calls your name. When the
transformation you are undergoing is more subtle in texture,
like saying goodbye to an old habit, Moldavite will help you
align with your new reality. Or try Shungite, Moss Agate
or Tugtupite.

FORGIVENESS

Dioptase   Whether you need to be kinder to yourself or let go
of hurt that someone else has caused you, forgiveness doesn't
happen all at once. It's a process that you set in motion. Finding
forgiveness requires self-love, self-worth and understanding.
Dioptase can help you practice forgiveness by supporting you
with its gentle and loving vibrations. You could also turn to
Black Moonstone, Rhodochrosite or Pink Tourmaline.

WISDOM
AND FREEDOM

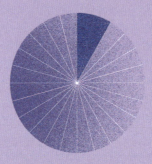

Sagittarius season is represented by the archer who shoots high and blazes a trail into new territory. The archer is also a centaur – half horse and half human, half wild and half philosophical. Sagittarius season is a time to feel fiercely alive and simultaneously inspired to ask big, existential questions. It's a season for expanding your boundaries and traveling physically and mentally to understand more about the world and the human experience.

GEMINI HOROSCOPE
FOR SAGITTARIUS SEASON

Take stock of your most important relationships. The Sun is drawing your attention to themes of communication and harmony. Is there something that's been left unsaid? If so, consider how you might communicate this in a gentle and considerate way. It is an excellent time to set boundaries, make amends, or arrive at a new resolution. Enjoy your meaningful partnerships.

Morning Practice

Go for a walk or
a jog out in nature.

Evening Practice

Memorize an
inspiring quote.

CRYSTALS FOR
SAGITTARIUS SEASON

INNER WISDOM

Azurite   In Sagittarius season, the archer knows that the best
way to take aim is to trust your inner wisdom. When you are
connected to your true self, it's easier to make choices. Life
feels more satisfying. Azurite is the stone to hold and carry
when you want to bolster your self-confidence and tune into
your wisdom. Or choose Idocrase, Shattuckite or Amethyst.

EXPANSION

Jasper   Ruled by the gas giant Jupiter, Sagittarius is the
sign of expansion. During this season, you can move beyond
anything that is limiting you. Is there an area of your life in
which you feel trapped in a cage? Maybe if you take a closer
look, you'll find that the door to the cage has been open the
entire time. Feel the freedom and expansion that is available
to you with the help of Jasper. This enlivening stone will help
you break out into new territory. Alternatives are Blue Topaz,
Pink Chalcedony or Ruby Iolite.

ADVENTURE AND TRAVEL

Turquoise   When you're setting out in search of new
horizons, reach for Turquoise as your talisman for protection
and luck. Travel and adventure require equal parts bravery
and boldness, but the reward is an expanded mindset and
perspective. Let Turquoise be your steady support system as
you push beyond your boundaries to discover excitement,
new opportunity and enlightenment. You could also use
Green Opal, Smoky Quartz or Aventurine.

CAREER
AND GOALS

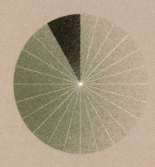

Like the mountain goat, in Capricorn season
you are primed to choose your footing carefully as
you make your ascent. Capricorn season brings practical
and productive forward motion. Use this energy efficiently
and tactically. You may choose to counterbalance this drive
and ambition with a large dose of acceptance, both
of yourself and others. Remember to give yourself a
break; you are trying your best.

GEMINI HOROSCOPE
FOR CAPRICORN SEASON

This is your season for letting go and making space for new beginnings. The Sun is putting pressure on the tricky topic of transformation. Trust is a key feature of transformation and change.

When you let go of what you know, can you trust that you'll be able to begin afresh? Go bravely into the season of change and discover how trust can help you navigate.

Affirmation
EVERY DAY, IN EVERY WAY, I AM GETTING BETTER.

Morning Practice	**Evening Practice**
Write down your goals.	Reflect on your accomplishments.

ACHIEVEMENT

Fluorite   Your Capricorn season recommendation supports
you in taking things one step at a time while staying focused
on your big picture goals. Look to Fluorite. Fluorite's unique
vibration can help you concentrate, while energizing you so
that you can keep moving forwards. Or look for support from
Ocean Jasper, Septarian Nodule or Tiger's Eye.

CAREER

Cat's Eye   Capricorn season is a wonderful time to take
stock. While you think about your work life, keep Cat's Eye by
your side. This stone helps you know your strengths, which is
imperative for a fulfilling career. It will help you feel optimistic
and believe in yourself. Cat's Eye's structured energy helps
you know your personal boundaries and make smart money
choices. You could also use Andradite Garnet, Apatite or
Hawk's Eye.

FOR SELF-ACCEPTANCE

Blue Aragonite   Let calming Blue Aragonite guide you
when you need to feel the soothing balm of self-acceptance.
Capricorn season pushes you to achieve, which may cause
you to question your progress in life. Counterbalance that by
learning to accept yourself for who you are. Blue Aragonite
has a compassionate energy that may inspire you to be less
judgemental towards yourself and show yourself more kindness.
Other crystals for self-acceptance are Prasiolite, Amethyst
or Shungite.

FRIENDSHIP AND VISION

Aquarius season pushes people and ideas to the forefront. What are your big ideas for the future? And who is in your community? Your vision for the future may also be a vision for humanity. Take the time to research causes to which you might contribute time, money and resources. Your friends, communities and social groups are extra important during this season, so prioritize the people who mean the most to you.

GEMINI HOROSCOPE
FOR AQUARIUS SEASON

The Sun is shining in the area of your chart that signifies expansion. If you want to expand, you need to believe that growth is possible. Optimism will help you get anywhere you want to go. Think about what helps you feel buoyant. Are there certain quotes or concepts that inspire you? Get yourself into a habit of thinking bigger and spark your sense of possibility.

FRIENDSHIP

Bismuth   Aquarius season asks you to turn towards your community. What can you offer? What will you receive? Friends enrich your life in so many ways, but mostly by encouraging your feeling of belonging – a natural mood booster. Bismuth has an expansive energy that helps you join with others in a shared sense of community. Carry Bismuth as a reminder that you are connected to others. Or you could reach for Carnelian, Sunset Sodalite or Blue Apatite.

FAITH IN THE FUTURE

Cavansite   The future is uncertain. Sometimes you need a boost to help you trust in the potential and possibility of what the future can become. In that case, reach for Cavansite. This stone has a sweet vibe of positivity that can give you the courage to believe in your biggest dreams for the future. Some alternatives are Peridot, Muscovite or Auralite 23.

VIBRATIONAL LIFT

Apophyllite   When Aquarius season asks you to turn your attention to what is possible, it helps to have a positive outlook. Without suppressing any challenging feelings (those are important and need to be processed), pay some special attention to the positive things in your life and work to create an enduring, positive mindset. If you need a little extra support, reach for Clear or Green Apophyllite. This high-vibe crystal can lift your spirits and help you feel full of potential. You could also try Quartz, Hematite or Angelite.

71

INTUITION AND SPIRITUALITY

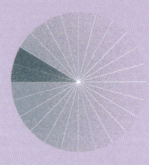

The most mystical season of all, Pisces season is the time to tune into your intuition. Slide like a slippery fish into the sphere of your dreams, faith, spirituality, compassion and creativity. This is a moment to rest, reflect and look inwards. Reconnect with your imagination. Feel your feelings. Plug into your spirituality or whatever makes you feel connected to the universe.

GEMINI HOROSCOPE FOR PISCES SEASON

While everyone else is caught up in the midst of emotional Pisces season, the Sun is lighting up your zone of concrete goals and ambitions. To work with this contradictory energy, tune into your feelings and use them as the inspiration for your objectives and strategies. Make a solid plan that feels completely authentic and aligned.

Morning Practice	**Evening Practice**
Record your dreams.	Do some freewriting to clear your mind.

CRYSTALS FOR PISCES SEASON

COMPASSION

Lavender Quartz   Lavender Quartz helps you feel peace and understanding for others. It will bestow upon you the softness that you need to open up to other people's perspectives. It will also allow you to dissolve drama with a heightened sense of empathy. This soothing and healing stone can offer strength while you stand in someone else's shoes. A compassionate life is a fulfilling life. As an alternative, turn to Thulite, Prehnite with Epidote or Fluorite.

INTUITION

Pink Opal   When you trust your inner guidance system you have ultimate clarity. Harness the power of your intuition in Pisces season with the help of Pink Opal. This stone will help you connect to yourself and to your guides. It raises the volume on your inner 'Yes' or 'No' by quietening any distractions and helping you connect within. Other crystals for intuition are Clear Quartz, Moldavite or Dumortierite.

FOR FAITH

Celestite   Faith can be thought of as a complete trust or confidence in someone or something. With a little bit of faith you may find it easier to contend with fear or anxiety. But trust and faith must be developed from within. In Pisces season, harness the power of high-vibrational Celestite to help you move beyond unnecessary fears as you put your trust in something bigger. You could also use Vatican Stone, Apophyllite or Turquoise.

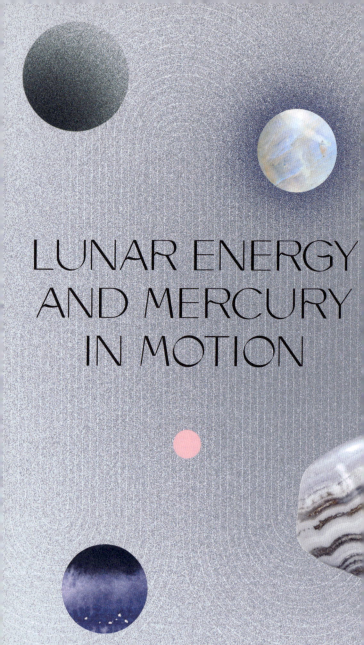

LUNAR ENERGY AND MERCURY IN MOTION

THE LUNAR CYCLE

In astrology, the Moon is a catalyst, helping us to move forwards with our goals and intentions.

The 29-day lunar cycle begins in darkness. The Moon then appears as a faint crescent and grows bigger until it's full. This process, from darkness to Full Moon, mirrors the incubation and development of your own creative process. Then, the Moon wanes until it completely disappears, reflecting another stage of the creative cycle – the process of releasing your efforts and making space for another cycle to begin. This allows new thoughts and ideas to emerge.

Each of the eight phases of the Moon cycle offers a different type of energy, which we will explore in this chapter. You can follow the Moon through the lunar month with crystal recommendations, setting your intentions in alignment with the New Moon and letting the lunar cycle help you make that intention into reality. The lunar cycle will also help you cleanse and release so that you can gently transition into the next phase.

By using crystals to work with the lunar cycle you can activate the potential of the Moon and amplify its energy. Through visualization or meditation, tap into the unique energies of each stage of the Moon cycle with the following crystals. For the suggested rituals at each phase, choose a crystal from the recommended options, or substitute with your favourite crystal.

Sun

New Moon

Waxing Crescent

Waning Crescent

First Quarter

Third Quarter

Earth

Waxing Gibbous

Waning Gibbous

Full Moon

SET YOUR NEW INTENTIONS

The Moon is dark. This is a time for reflection and a time to connect with your inner self. Use your energy to envision what you would like to make happen. What do you desire? What are your dreams? Anything is possible – imagine that you are planting seeds of intention that will manifest and grow throughout the Waxing Moon Phase. The New Moon is a quiet and emotional time and you may discover that, as you think about what you would like to create, many different feelings arise. Excitement, anticipation, fear, worry – whatever feelings arise, make space for those feelings and be gentle with yourself. Listen to your intuition and imagine your next steps.

Black Moonstone can support you during the delicate and sensitive New Moon vibration. It offers wellsprings o patience and peace as you work with your emotions and reflect on your life When your dreams are germinating under the surface, Black Moonstone can help you trust your own process.

Labradorite opens your third eye wide so that you can tune into your intuition and design your goals in accordance with your path and purpose.

Pink Sapphire's loving energy can buffer you and help you feel emotionally at ease.

Ametrine provides sweet joy and concentrated focus so that you can set intentions with confidence.

TRUST,
INSPIRATION, SERENITY
AND DELIGHT

New Moon Ritual

Freewrite about what you yearn for and anything else that's on your mind. Then jot down your intentions for this Moon cycle on a piece of paper and place your chosen crystal on top.

NURTURE YOUR INTENTIONS

ur seeds of intention are germinating nder the soil, and maybe some of the ants are just beginning to sprout. As e lunar energy builds momentum, ake sure that you have the resources u need to achieve your goals. Provide ructure and support for yourself. This cle is just beginning to take shape, consider how your choices will etermine your direction – maybe there e changes you'd like to make to your als. Remain curious throughout this ocess, because anything is possible!

Turquoise is a powerhouse of a crystal that can deftly carry you through the precarious Waxing Crescent phase. At this moment you need a subtle combination of confidence, discernment, curiosity and commitment. Turquoise can help you understand the truth of what you need to create, and it can help you stay open and accepting of your process. Use this stone as you decide what you really want to manifest and commit to during this Moon cycle.

Shattuckite helps you intuitively illuminate your path so that you can make the decisions that are right for you.

Pyrite offers crystalline protection and is a wonderful choice to help you realize your goals.

Orange Calcite gives you mental focus and lots of energy for the journey ahead.

TRUTH,
NTUITION, MANIFESTATION
AND FOCUS

Waxing Crescent Moon Ritual

Read and rewrite your intentions for this Moon cycle.
Decorate the paper and place your chosen crystal back on top.

BUILD YOUR MOMENTUM

Look around your garden of intentions and discover what is growing. Have your goals started to take shape? If so, how are they coming along? Do you need more support? Perhaps you have had surprising results? At the First Quarter Moon the constraints of reality can be intimidating. You have big dreams, but sometimes you encounter resistance when dreams make contact with real world limitations. Maybe there is more work required than you had foreseen, or there are real-world issues with time, money, support or other resources. Give yourself lots of encouragement. Pivot, and reassess if necessary. This is an exciting, high energy time, so keep taking action and building momentum.

Bumblebee Jasper When reality, and all of its limitations, hits, Bumblebee Jasper can help you stay the course with confidence. Lean on this crystal when you need the energy to just keep moving forwards. It will subdue your fears and inspire you to push past your comfort zone.

Peridot is a cheery companion that will help you look at any situation with optimism.

Tangerine Quartz offers creative potential that makes problem solving effortless.

Aventurine will vitalize you and give you the confidence to keep going.

CONFIDENCE,
OPTIMISM, CREATIVITY AND
VITALITY

First Quarter Moon Ritual

Light a candle, hold your chosen crystal and
visualize your intentions being realized.

DEVELOP YOUR INTENTIONS

s astonishing what a little effort can eate! Now that you've made it to the axing Gibbous phase of the Moon cle, you are starting to see the effects the intentions that you set. If your al was to improve your nutrition, you ay be feeling better already. If you t motivated to get out there and start ting, you may have started some new nversations. Whatever the last few ys have revealed, now is the time to ll up your sleeves and actively give ape to your garden. What will you ed out? What is working, and what n't working? What changes might you ake? The intensity has almost peaked take tender care of your emotional ell-being as you keep putting in effort wards your dreams.

Jet Jet's grounding energy will help you establish deep root systems for your developing intentions. When you need strength and motivation to keep pushing forwards with your goals, this stone will support you. As a bonus, jet has a sheltering vibration that can steady you emotionally and help you surge forwards with optimism and hope.

Hematite offers balance and protection, helping you proactively take care of yourself during this active time.

Carnelian lights your fire with sparkling enthusiasm and convinces you to tune into your creative side.

Blue Lace Agate calms your mind, allowing you to weed through your options and make solid decisions.

GROUNDING,
PROTECTION, ENTHUSIASM
AND PEACE OF MIND

Waxing Gibbous Moon Ritual

While holding or wearing your chosen crystal, do something that feels active or expressive, such as dancing, painting, gardening, cooking or singing. Imagine your goals and repeat your intentions.

HARVEST

Everything is revealed under the light of the Moon. The attempts you've made, your wins, your losses. It's time to get out in the garden and harvest the crop. Regardless of whether the bounty lives up to your expectations, there is something to appreciate and celebrate. At the Full Moon, honour what you've created and give gratitude to yourself for your commitment. This phase represents the push and pull of two opposite energies as the Moon is in the opposite sign to the Sun. The result is a highly polarized and intense energy that can heighten emotions, pull you in two different directions, or cause you to realize something important. Make sure to be very gentle with yourself and those around you.

White Moonstone symbolizes the Full Moon and all of its glorious creativity and excitement. This pearly white crystal shines a bright light so that you can see clearly. As you examine the fruits that you've cultivated during the Waxing Moon phase, use the receptive and healing energy of White Moonstone to help you accept and celebrate. It's time for gratitude, and this comforting crystal will help you open up to that feeling.

Green Apatite is an antidote to the drama of the Full Moon – use it to highlight joy and abundance.

Jade has a subtle, soothing energy that imparts an optimistic attitude.

Stilbite connects the heart, mind and intuition – this can help you rationally balance your emotions while still opening up to divine insight.

EMOTIONAL EXPLORATION, ABUNDANCE, PEACEFULNESS AND RECEPTIVITY

Full Moon Ritual

Hold your chosen crystal and write down three things that you are grateful for. The Full Moon is also a great time to cleanse your crystals. Place them outside or on a windowsill and let them bathe in the Moon's healing energy.

REFLECT AND REVIEW

ow that the intensity of the full reveal
as begun to wane, you can settle
eeper into your new reality. Indulge
urself and enjoy. As the Moon has
oved through waxing to waning, this
the beginning of a less active and
ore receptive phase. This means that
u can simply sit with the ebbing
llness of what is. Begin a process of
ompassionate review. What have you
arned? What will you do differently in
e next Moon cycle? Each lunar cycle
veals an older, more experienced
rsion of who you are becoming. So
nk into this moment of reflection and
t to know yourself once more.

Obsidian offers a protective energy
that buffers and supports. Use it at the
Waning Gibbous phase of the Moon
cycle to release the past and securely
recline into the experience of the
moment. Obsidian's cleansing vibes
can help you remove any junk from
your thought patterns, allowing you to
think from a new perspective. Harness
its clarifying energy to appraise your
situation with equanimity and objectivity.

Tiger's Eye is for encouragement and
strength as you review your progress and
make plans for improvement.

Citrine offers joy and optimism so that
you can look at your accomplishments
through a positive lens.

Celestite provides tranquillity as
you come down off the high of the
Full Moon.

_____

PROTECTION,
STRENGTH, JOY AND
TRANQUILLITY

_____

Waning Gibbous Moon Ritual

Pour yourself some tea, water, or other drink of your
choice, and take the time to sit and quietly appreciate the
moment. With your chosen crystal nearby, review your
intention and gratitude lists.

LET GO

Get comfortable letting go so that you can make space for new things. At the Last Quarter Moon allow the leaves to fall and the fading plants to return to the soil. A tree drops its leaves to conserve resources. Take stock of what you want to let go of, so that you can use your energy wisely. Is there someone you need to forgive? Do you need to release your expectations and accept something about your life? Release the past or an outdated way of thinking, let go and forgive. Maybe you declutter your closet, acknowledge your reality, admit your mistakes, get really honest with yourself, or forgive yourself or others. The Last Quarter Moon asks that you put in a little effort to let go of the emotions and ideas that are taking up excess energy.

LOVE, SUPPORT, GROUNDING AND GENTLE SELF-REFLECTION

Rose Quartz is an emotional balm that can help you forgive yourself and others. As the Last Quarter Moon inspires you to release your expectatio and accept your current reality, you need a soothing support that helps you open up compassionately. Rose Quart brings playful, loving vibes and helps you gently accept a situation and move forwards.

Rutilated Quartz offers a powerful support in following through on your intentions as you review what you've learned and plan for the next phase.

Smoky Quartz provides grounding, protection and assistance in clearing t thoughts and feelings that you are rea to release.

Amethyst is for gently releasing old mental patterns and contemplating new possibilities.

Last Quarter Moon Ritual

Create a peaceful environment and run a bath for yourself. Place a water-safe, non-toxic crystal (such as Quartz or Amethyst) in the bath while you review your intentions from this moon cycle. Repeat these affirmations, 'I make space for clarity' and 'I release the past'.

STILLNESS AND REST

he lunar energy is encouraging you
» turn inwards and be still. All is quiet
a the winter of your metaphorical
arden. Embracing stillness offers
iany benefits. By allowing your inner
andscape to exist without judgement,
ou honour who you are now. Slowing
own can also help you uncover your
alues and emotional truth – which
iay not be so apparent when you are
asily running around. And last but
ot least, rest and quiet will help you
echarge your energy for the next cycle.
hallenge yourself to slow down and be
resent in the moment. There will be
mple time for new plans and dreams
hen the next cycle begins.

Serpentine can help you open a
gateway to the stillness within and
to the profound interconnectedness
of the universe. Using this crystal
during your Waning Crescent Moon
meditations will help you feel buffered
and supported in the understanding
that there is no-one you need to be and
nothing you need to do. Float along
with the waves of existence. You'll know
when the time is right again for action.

Selenite radiates cleansing energy that
can help you release the past cycle and
prepare to make a fresh start.

Howlite soothes your spirit and
quietens any absurd complaints from
your 'inner critic'.

Aquamarine helps you create a
meditative state of mind so that you can
listen to the stillness within.

CONNECTION WITH
NATURE, CLEANSING,
SOOTHING AND REFLECTION

Waning Crescent Moon Ritual

Sit quietly in the meditation of your choosing. Hold your
crystal or place it nearby.

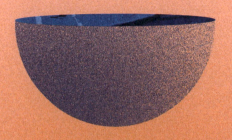

MERCURY
RETROGRADE

Mercury Retrograde deserves attention as it's a chance to review your plans and goals. It's notoriously known for causing technology and communication issues, but the upside of this time period is that it offers an invitation to slow down and re-assess where you are and where you want to go.

Fast-moving Mercury symbolizes connection, communication and technology. Mercury is the part of you that learns, thinks, teaches and talks.

Mercury orbits the Sun about four times as fast as the Earth and every time that Mercury zips past the Earth an optical illusion occurs that makes it look as though Mercury is moving backwards. When Mercury appears to be moving backwards (Mercury Retrograde), it's a great opportunity to slow down. Go back over your thoughts and decisions of recent months and review them. Turn inwards to gain guidance from your intuition.

Mercury Retrograde happens about three times a year and lasts for about three weeks each time. You can use these retrograde periods as a moment to check in with yourself and review your practices, thoughts and relationships. Have you been putting off an uncomfortable conversation? Is there something that you need to be honest about with yourself when it comes to relationships, work or money? What has your body been trying to tell you? Is there some new way that you could step out of your comfort zone? What would help you feel more secure and supported?

Underlying issues tend to rise to the surface during Mercury Retrograde. It's typically advised to make sure that you are extra clear in your communications during these periods, and that you wait until the retrograde period has ended before beginning new projects or signing contracts. But it's an excellent time to pick up where you left off on something – to rethink, redo and review.

YOUR CRYSTAL PRACTICE DURING MERCURY RETROGRADE

Crystal energy can help you slow down your busy mind and tune into your intuition during Mercury Retrograde. As you rethink and review, these crystals will amplify your intuition and clarity.

KEEN INSIGHT

Pietersite   Employ this speckled Quartz for illuminated insight paired with steady determination.

CLARITY AND COMMUNICATION

Aquamarine   This stone soothes and calms the mind while simultaneously boosting your ability to communicate clearly.

CREATIVE THOUGHT

Citrine   A crystal that spurs your imagination, helping you conceptualize how you might like patterns or situations to change.

Beginning of Mercury Retrograde Ritual	End of Mercury Retrograde Ritual
Perform a full and gentle review of the issues most affecting you by writing a journal entry using the following prompt: 'What do I need to see that I'm not seeing when it comes to my …' Give yourself lots of gratitude in the process and call on your chosen crystal to provide understanding and clarity. When you've finished, write down three takeaways on a small piece of paper and place your crystal on top of it for the remainder of the Retrograde. Drawing on the power of your crystal, let your subconscious mind continue to explore and reveal the subtleties of these thoughts and questions over the coming weeks.	Near the end of the Retrograde cycle, set an intention to integrate what you've learned during the past days and weeks. Begin by returning to your piece of paper and your crystal. What came up for you during Mercury Retrograde? Was there a new realization, attitude or interest that emerged? Think about what you may have realized and journal about what you'd like to bring into your life now. Is there an intention (see page 22) or affirmation that could come from this exploration? If so, write it down. Look in a mirror and repeat your intention or affirmation five times while holding your crystal. Remember to thank your crystal and to thank yourself for showing up. For the next two weeks, repeat this daily ritual.

CONCLUSION

This book has taken you deep below the Earth's surface, through the metaphorical caverns of crystals and their symbolism. You've connected the dots of the solar system and the meaning of the astrology you were born with. By pairing the forces of the stars above with the crystals below, you've gained tools that can help you navigate your unique journey with wisdom.

In Part Two, you learned about the crystals that can support your unique astrology. This section included insights for Gemini Sun, Moon and Rising signs, along with supportive crystal recommendations for what your sign needs in five key life areas.

Life is always changing and so in Part Three you learned to follow the energy of the Sun as it moves on its annual journey through the zodiac, finding crystals that may help you elaborate on the theme of each astrological season.

Revolving and evolving with changing astrological cycles continued in Part Four, where you paired crystal energy with the ebb and flow of the Moon, and learned to harness the power of crystals in tandem with Mercury Retrograde to perform a trimonthly check-in.

All the answers are already within you. When you choose a crystal, you awaken the vibration of that crystal within yourself. Harness your astro-crystal practice to help you see what already exists inside of you. You have everything you need.

With the cosmos above and the crystals below, you are always connected and supported. Let the stones and the stars strengthen your self-awareness and self-trust as you continue your crystalline cosmic journey.

Crystals and astrology are not intended to be a substitute for medical advice, diagnosis or treatment. Always seek the advice of your qualified healthcare provider.

RESOURCES

GET YOUR BIRTH CHART	www.sandysitron.com/crystals
ASTROLOGY READING	www.sandysitron.com
CRYSTALS	*101 Power Crystals: The Ultimate Guide to Magical Crystals, Gems, and Stones for Healing and Transformation* Judy Hall
CRYSTAL ENERGY HEALING	https://www.kalisaaugustine.com/
SOURCING CRYSTALS RESPONSIBLY	moonrisecrystals.com/
SPIRAL CRYSTALS	spiralcrystals.com/
HOOF AND PAW	hoofandpawuk.com/
ASTROLOGY	*Astrology for Yourself* Demetra George and Douglas Bloch
AFFIRMATION WORK	Transformational coach Dana Balicki: https://danabalicki.com/
AFFIRMATION WORK	*Empowerment: The Art of Creating Your Life as You Want It* Gail Straub and David Gershon
ASTROLOGY EDUCATION	www.thestrology.com
	Ritual Enchantments *A Modern Witch's Guide to Self-Possession* Mya Spalter

FEATURED CRYSTALS

Agate 31
Agatized Coral 55
Amethyst 15, 84
Ametrine 63, 78
Apophyllite 47, 71
Aquamarine 44, 55, 85, 89
Aventurine 80
Azurite 67
Bismuth 71
Black Moonstone 78
Blue Aragonite 69
Blue Calcite 57
Blue Lace Agate 38, 81
Bornite 57
Bumblebee Jasper 80
Carnelian 10, 81
Cat's Eye 69

Cavansite 71
Celestite 73, 83
Chevron Amethyst 61
Chrysocolla 40
Citrine 45, 83, 89
Clear Quartz 14, 41, 61
Dioptase 65
Fire Agate 51
Fluorite 69
Girasol Quartz 41
Golden Apatite 59
Green Apatite 53, 82
Green Jade 53
Heliodor 55
Hematite 81
Hessonite Garnet 51
Howlite 85
Iolite 63

Jade 82
Jasper 67
Jet 81
Labradorite 78
Lavender Quartz 73
Moldavite 65
Moss Agate 39
Obsidian 83
Orange Calcite 79
Peridot 80
Pietersite 89
Pink Aventurine 51
Pink Mangano Calcite 57
Pink Opal 73
Pink Sapphire 78
Pyrite 79
Rose Quartz 10, 14
Rutilated Quartz, 41

Selenite 13, 25, 85
Serpentine 85
Shattuckite 79
Shungite 63
Smoky Quartz 13, 84
Stilbite 82
Stromatolite 61
Red Jasper 53
Red Tourmaline 65
Rose Quartz 84
Rutilated Quartz 59, 84
Tangerine Quartz 80
Thulite 43, 59
Tiger's Eye 46, 83
Turquoise 67, 79
White Moonstone 82

LAURENCE KING

First published in Great Britain in 2022 by Laurence King
an imprint of The Orion Publishing Group Ltd
Carmelite House, 50 Victoria Embankment
London EC4Y 0DZ

An Hachette UK Company

10 9 8 7 6 5 4 3 2 1

A CIP catalogue record for this book is
available from the British Library.

ISBN 978-0-8578-2926-9

Design: Therese Vandling

Printed in China by C&C Offset Printing Co. Ltd

Laurence King Publishing is committed to ethical and
sustainable production. We are proud participants in the
Book Chain Project®. [bookchainproject.com]

**BOOK
CHAIN
PROJECT**

www.laurenceking.com
www.orionbooks.co.uk